# STRANGER FILLINGS

# STRANGER FILLINGS

## THE MUFFIN BROTHERS

TRAPEZE

First published in Great Britain in 2017 by Trapeze,
an imprint of The Orion Publishing Group Ltd
Carmelite House, 50 Victoria Embankment,
London EC4Y 0DZ

An Hachette UK company

10 9 8 7 6 5 4 3 2 1

A CIP catalogue record for this book is
available from the British Library.

ISBN (Hardback) 978 1409 1 7335 9

Printed in Italy

www.orionbooks.co.uk

TO DAD —
ONLY IN
PASSING

# CONTENTS

INTRODUCTION 8

WHAT YOU WILL NEED 10

DIFFICULTY RATING 12

DEMOGORGONZOLA TARTLETS 16

D&D DELIGHTS 20

HOPPER'S COFFEE & CONTEMPLATION 24

BENNY'S BURGER 30

BARB'S MYSTERY DIP 34

LIGHT BITES 38

BRENNER BISCUITS 44

EL'S COLA CRUSH 48

JOYCE'S CLOSE CALL 53

WILL'S FAKE CAKE 64

CAKE BYERS 68

JANE IVES' DELICIOUS DIVE 72

EL'S TELEPATHIC TART
    (WITH RUSSIAN DRESSING)    80
FRIENDSHIP BITES    84
EL FLOTANTE    88

MONSTER-HUNTING MEDLEY    94
ELEVEN'S EGGOS    98
MIKE'S ROCK CAKE RESCUE    103

FRIENDS DON'T LI(M)E PIE    110
THE UPSIDE DOWN CAKE    114
WILL'S SLUG SURPRISE    120

AUTHOR'S NOTE    126
WITH THANKS TO...    127
ABOUT THE AUTHORS    128

# INTRO

There is another world.
A world where the trees look
like spoons. Where the rivers
run red with jam and the sky is
darkened in a blizzard of
sugar.
In 1984, two brothers made their
way into this alternate,
deliciously doughy netherworld.
This is their story...

Stranger Fillings

STRANGER FILLINGS

Do you know the difference between a slingshot and a wrist rocket?

Here are some essential items you will need on your quest.

# DIFFICULTY

When you're about to embark on a ten-hour campaign into the Vale of Shadows you'd better know what you're doing...

Use this symbol to gauge the level of difficulty of each recipe:

## EASY

'Mouth-breather'

## MEDIUM

'Sometimes your total obliviousness just blows my mind'

## HARD

'You're stealthy, like a ninja!'

# DEMOGORGON-ZOLA TARTLETS

'**Today we make contact**' **with this monster of a snack**

## INGREDIENTS

1 packet ready-to-roll puff pastry
150g Gorgonzola cheese (Danish Blue is also a good
  alternative)

TO DECORATE
3–4 figs
1 jar of olives
Pine nuts, chopped

You will need: a man-shaped cutter

FEEDS

# DIRECTIONS

Clear the work surface of any spilt blood before beginning.

Preheat the oven to 200°C (180°C fan/400°F/gas mark 6).

Roll out the puff pastry and use the cutter to make a rough outline.

Trim round the body shape with a sharp knife and remove the head.
Use excess strips of puff pastry to fashion claws on the hands and feet.

Crumble the Gorgonzola over the pastry and use a knife to spread over
the body.

Bake the tart in the oven for 20 minutes, until golden.

Meanwhile, use a sharp knife to trim the top of the fig and score into
quarters without cutting all the way through. Open the fig up to make
the demogorgon's flower-shaped head.

Use a knife to cut a black olive into 2cm slices and place a slice in the
centre of the fig head. Cut the pine nuts into small, jagged pieces and
dress the black olive as shown.

Remove the tart from the oven and arrange with the fig head.

Enjoy. Just be aware that as you soon as you touch this dish things
are going to get very bad, very quickly.

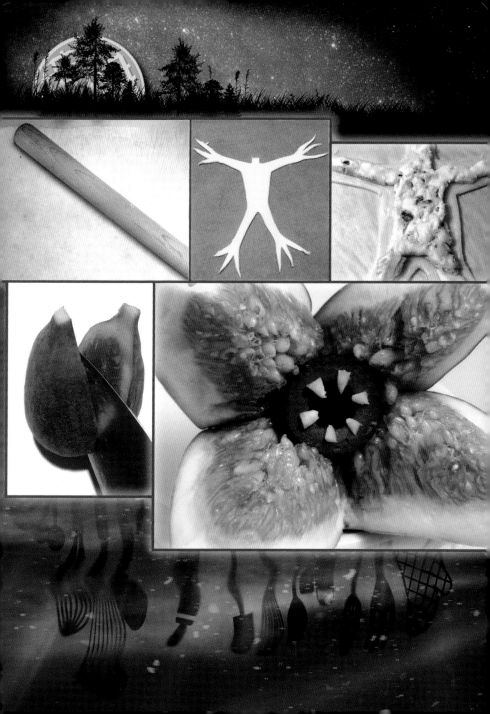

DIFFICULTY

## Roll the dice with this deliciously retro recipe

## Ingredients

**TO MAKE THE BISCUITS**
500g/1lb 2oz plain flour
400g/14oz butter, firm
200g/7oz icing sugar
4 egg yolks
2 tsp vanilla extract

**TO DECORATE**
200g/7oz icing sugar
2 egg whites
Black and red food colours

**TO MAKE THE COUNTER**
80g/3oz milk chocolate
Flaked almonds
Hundreds and thousands
Sugar sprinkles
Milk chocolate buttons

You will need: a hexagon biscuit cutter, a piping bag and a small plain nozzle.

FEEDS

# DIRECTIONS

## TO MAKE THE BISCUITS:

Put the flour in a bowl. Cut the butter into small pieces and add to the flour. Rub the butter into the flour with your fingertips until the mix looks like breadcrumbs.

Add the sugar, egg yolks and vanilla extract and mix to form a dough. Put into a plastic bag and chill for at least 30 minutes.

Roll out the dough on a lightly floured surface to about 5mm (0.25 inch) thickness. Cut out shapes with a cutter and place them on a baking sheet lined with baking parchment. Put back into the fridge to chill again for 30 minutes.

Meanwhile, preheat the oven to 180°C (160°C fan/350°F/gas mark 4). Bake the biscuits for 12–15 minutes. Remove from the oven and allow to cool on the baking sheet before carefully lifting off.

## TO DECORATE:

Sieve the icing sugar into a small bowl and add some little egg white, little by little, beating well until a piping consistency is reached. With a piping bag fitted with a small plain nozzle (or small paper piping bag with the end cut off), pipe the outline sections of the dice onto the individual biscuits.

Loosen the texture of the icing with a little water. Divide into thirds and colour them three different shades of red, as shown. Carefully fill the shapes using a small teaspoon.

Once completely dried, use a paintbrush to apply the white food colour numbers.

## TO MAKE THE COUNTER:

Place the chocolate in a heatproof bowl and set over a pan of simmering water, stirring occasionally until just melted. Use a piping bag with a small nozzle to pipe the shape on to baking parchment as shown in the photo opposite. Insert the almonds and sugar sprinkles as shown and leave in the freezer to cool. Use a little melted chocolate to affix the counter to a chocolate button as a base.

Your quest is over. If you are looking for a new challenge, why not try to create something that looks a bit like a giant spider?

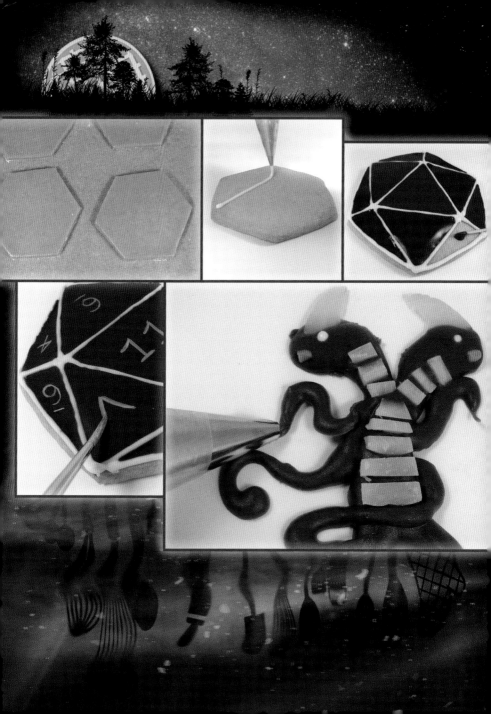

# HOPPER'S COFFEE & CONTEMPLATION

With a hint of caffeine and alcohol, this is a dish to remember, with booze to help you forget

## INGREDIENTS

**FOR THE CUPCAKES**
100g/4oz butter, softened
100g/4oz caster sugar
2 medium eggs, lightly beaten
125g/4½oz self-raising flour
1 tsp baking powder
1 tsp coffee liquor (just enough to
    kick-start your day)

**FOR THE BUTTERCREAM**
250g/10oz icing sugar
125g/5oz butter, softened
1–2 tbsp milk
Pink food colour

**TO DECORATE**
Half-covered chocolate biscuits
50g/2oz milk chocolate
Chocolate sticks
White chocolate buttons
Black and red food colour
25g/1oz white chocolate
Red sugar balls
Chocolate sprinkles
Yellow chocolate stars (you are the
    chief, after all)
Blue hard-shelled sweets

You will need: paper cases

## FEEDS

24

# DIRECTIONS

Get off the couch, brush your teeth, have a smoke and a swig of beer, and get on with it.

Preheat the oven to 180°C (160°C fan/350°F/gas mark 4). Place six large paper cases into muffin or bun tin.

Put all the cupcake ingredients into a mixing bowl and whisk well together, first with a wooden spoon, then with a whisk until properly mixed and smooth.

With an ice-cream scoop or a large spoon, divide the mix among the paper cases and bake for 15–20 minutes until the tops are golden. Transfer to a rack to cool completely before decorating.

Whisk the icing sugar and butter together in a free-standing electric mixer with a paddle attachment on medium-slow speed until they come together and are well mixed.

Turn the mixer up to medium-high and continue whisking for at least five minutes until light and fluffy. Add a little of the pink food colour with a teaspoon and mix well until the desired colour is reached. Spoon or pipe the icing on top of the cold cakes. Store in the fridge to cool.

To create a hat, use a knife to carve one of the spare cupcakes into the mound of a hat. Place the shaped cake on top of a half-covered chocolate biscuit.

Meanwhile, melt the milk chocolate very gently over hot water and once melted use a knife to coat the cupcake and the biscuit, so they fuse together. Place in the fridge to cool.

Use a sharp knife to cut the chocolate sticks to make the eyebrows and cut the white chocolate buttons to make the eyes. Use a paintbrush to apply the black and red food colours to paint the eyes as shown.

To make the cigarette, use a length of chocolate stick and apply melted white chocolate (made with the above technique) and the red sugar balls to form the lit end.

Take a cupcake out of the fridge and draw a line to form the mouth, using a paintbrush and the black food colour. Using a moistened toothpick, apply the chocolate sprinkles to create the beard and then insert the cigarette. Add the eyes and eyebrows and the hat from the fridge.

Affix a yellow chocolate star to a blue hard-shelled sweet using a dab of melted chocolate, and fasten to the cupcake case with melted chocolate.

Stand back and admire your work. And if all else fails, throw a punch.

# BENNY'S BURGER

## A sweet snack that didn't get its just desserts

### INGREDIENTS

Remember, if you want some food then
   you've got to talk first

1 packet lime gelatin jelly

FOR THE BUN
25g/1oz butter, softened
25g/1oz caster sugar
1 medium egg
25g/1oz self-raising flour
Vegetable oil
Sesame seeds

FOR THE REST OF THE BURGER
50g/2oz dark chocolate
Half-covered chocolate biscuits
Yellow-coloured chewy fruit sweets
Red piping gel
Edible paper
Red and blue food colour

You will need: a toothpick, a fine
paintbrush

FEEDS

30

# DIRECTIONS

Follow the instructions on the packet of jelly and pour a thin layer into a shallow baking tray and set aside to cool.

To make the bun, preheat the oven to 180°C (160°C fan/350°F/ gas mark 4). Line a muffin tin with a couple of cases. Put all the bun ingredients except the sesame seeds and vegetable oil (using only ½ an egg) into a bowl and whisk with a handheld electric mixer or wooden spoon until light and fluffy.

Divide the mix into the muffin cases. Bake for 10–15 minutes or until well risen, golden brown and firm to the touch. Allow to cool for a couple of minutes, then transfer the cupcakes to a wire rack to cool completely.

Use a knife to slice the top off both cupcakes. These will form the upper and lower buns of the burger. Use a little vegetable oil and a toothpick to apply the sesame seeds to the top bun.

To make the patties, melt the chocolate in a bowl suspended over a pan of simmering water (do not allow the bottom of the bowl to touch the water), then use a knife to cover the biscuits in the melted chocolate. Set aside on a rack to cool. Once cooled, place them on the burger bun.

To make the cheese, place the chewy fruit sweets on a micro-waveable plate and microwave for 1 minute or until melted. Remove from the microwave and once cool enough to handle tease it into the shape of the cheese and add to the burger.

Once the jelly has cooled, cut out a lettuce-shaped section and add to the burger. Repeat the assembly steps for a multi-tiered burger.

Use the red piping gel to create a tomato-sauce effect.

Use scissors to trim a flag from the edible paper and decorate using a paintbrush to apply the food colour.

Finally, use a sharp knife to cut a hole in the shape of a bullet wound into the top bun and add the red food colour for blood using a fine paintbrush.

Repeat these steps for a three-tiered burger.

Check that any guests who show up sound the same as they did on the phone...

# BARB'S MYSTERY DIP

## Easily overlooked, this sweet side-dish will be sorely missed once it's gone

### INGREDIENTS

Gelatin – enough for 2 pints of water
1 pack ice-cream wafers
Silver food spray
Liquorice laces
Liquorice tube
100g/4oz white chocolate
Some clear boiled sweets
Blue food colour
Red food colour
Orange food colour

You will need: a toothpick

## FEEDS

# DIRECTIONS

Prepare the gelatin as directed on the packet. Put it in the fridge
to speed up cooling, but don't let it set. Try not to think about Nancy
and Jonathan.

Use a knife to cut the wafers into the shape of a diving board; you may
need to stack two or three together to achieve the required strength.
Be careful not to cut your hand. That would be a big mistake right now.

Use silver food spray to paint the liquorice laces. Once dry, cut into short
lengths to form the diving-board handles.

Cut a small piece of liquorice tube to form the underside of the diving
board.

Melt the chocolate very gently over hot water and once melted, use a knife
to apply the chocolate and join the wafers together. Once dry, attach the
silver-painted laces to either side of the wafer as shown. Use more melted
chocolate to seal the wafers to the rim of the bowl or cup with the piece
of liquorice tube.

Hold in place until the chocolate cools and can support the diving-board
structure. (It's important to chill, Barb!)

Once cooled, pour the gelatin liquid into your chosen bowl or cup and
add blue food colour until the desired shade is achieved. Before the jelly
has fully set, mix some red food colouring with a little water and use a
toothpick to apply a couple of drops to the surface of the jelly.

To make the glasses, add the orange food colour to the white chocolate,
place in the piping bag and pipe the glasses shape on to some baking
parchment.

To make the broken glass, crush the boiled sweets to make flat shards.
Use a toothpick to insert them into the frames of the glasses, before the
chocolate cools.

Sit quietly and wait for the lights to go down... It's dinner time!

# LIGHT BITES

**There's nothing like this electrifying trio of cupcakes to bring family back together**

## INGREDIENTS

**FOR THE CUPCAKES**
100g/4oz butter, softened
100g/4oz caster sugar
2 medium eggs, lightly beaten
125g/4½oz self-raising flour
1 tsp baking powder

**FOR THE BUTTERCREAM**
250g/10oz icing sugar
125g/5oz butter, softened

**TO DECORATE**
3 packs hard-shelled sweets
50g/2oz milk chocolate

You will need: a large piping bag with medium-sized star-shaped nozzle and a small piping bag with a small cone-shaped nozzle (as well as around 100 table lamps scattered around your house)

## FEEDS

# DIRECTIONS

Get out the Christmas box from the attic.

Preheat the oven to 180°C (160°C fan/350°F/gas mark 4). Place six large paper cases into a muffin or bun tin.

Put all the cupcake ingredients into a mixing bowl and whisk well together, first with a wooden spoon, then with a whisk until properly mixed and smooth.

With an ice-cream scoop or a large spoon, divide the mix among the paper cases and bake for 15–20 minutes until the tops are golden. Transfer to a rack to cool completely before decorating.

Whisk the icing sugar and butter together in a free-standing electric mixer with a paddle attachment on a medium-slow speed until they come together and are well mixed.

Turn the mixer up to medium-high and continue whisking for at least 5 minutes until light and fluffy.

Use a large piping bag with a star-shaped nozzle to pipe the buttercream on to the cupcakes in a swirl pattern.

Melt the milk chocolate very gently over hot water and once melted use the small piping bag and nozzle to create the wiring for the lights.

Apply a selection of the hard-shelled sweets to form the pattern of lights along the chocolate wiring.

Stand back and watch the light show. Remember, one blink for 'yes' and two for 'no'.

# BRENNER BISCUITS

## Once you Papa you can't stop!

## INGREDIENTS

**FOR THE BISCUITS**
500g/18oz plain flour
400g/14oz butter, firm
200g/7oz icing sugar
4 medium egg yolks
2 tsp vanilla extract

**TO DECORATE**
200g/7oz icing sugar
2 medium egg whites
Black food colour

**FOR THE MERINGUE**
200g/7oz caster sugar
1 medium egg white
¼ tsp cream of tartar
75ml water
Pinch salt
2 tsp vanilla extract

You will need: a gingerbread man cutter, a piping bag with nozzle and a toothpick but no parenting skills whatsoever.

## FEEDS

44

# DIRECTIONS

Put the flour in a bowl. Cut the butter into small pieces and add to the flour.

Rub the butter into the flour with your fingertips until the mix looks like breadcrumbs.

Add the sugar, egg yolks and vanilla extract and mix to form a dough. Put into a plastic bag and chill for at least 30 minutes.

Roll out the dough on a lightly floured surface to about 5mm (¼ inch) thickness. Cut out shapes with a 'gingerbread man' cutter and place them on a baking sheet lined with baking parchment. Fold the arms as shown. Put back into the fridge to chill again for 30 minutes.

Meanwhile, preheat the oven to 180°C (160°C fan/350°F/gas mark 4). Bake the biscuits for 12–15 minutes, until they are beginning to brown around the edges. Remove from the oven and allow to cool on the sheet before carefully lifting off.

Sieve the icing sugar into a small bowl and add some egg white, little by little, beating well until a piping consistency is reached. Divide into two quantities, one twice as big as the other, and use the black food colour to colour the larger set dark grey and the smaller set light grey.

With a piping bag fitted with a small plain nozzle (or small paper piping bag with the end cut off), pipe the outline of the jacket and shirt. Loosen the texture of the light grey icing with a little water, then carefully fill in the jacket shape using a small teaspoon and a toothpick. Allow to set.

Ask your daughter to kill a cat and watch as she fails. You're not angry, you're just disappointed.

To make the meringue, whisk the sugar, egg whites, cream of tartar, salt and 75ml water in a heatproof bowl. Put the bowl over a saucepan of simmering water and whisk with a handheld electric mixer on a low speed, then gradually increase the speed to high and whisk until soft peaks form. This will take 5–10 minutes. Remove the bowl from the saucepan and continue whisking until the meringue is fluffy. Add the vanilla. With a piping bag fitted with a star nozzle, pipe the meringue mix on the biscuits for hair.

As you tuck in, take pride in the fact that your 'daughter' has the power to kill people with her mind.

# EL'S COLA CRUSH

**Test your powers of concentration
with some experimental eating**

## INGREDIENTS

**FOR THE CUPCAKES**
1 egg
120ml/4fl oz milk
4 tbsp vegetable oil
200g/7oz plain flour
100g/3½oz caster sugar
2 tsp baking powder
⅛ tsp salt

**FOR THE BUTTERCREAM**
125g/5oz butter, softened
250g/10oz icing sugar
1–2 tbsp milk
Pink food colour

**TO DECORATE**
Chocolate sprinkles
Liquorice laces
White food colour
Strawberry laces
Mini marshmallows
Black food colour
White chocolate buttons
60g/2oz melted chocolate
Purple food colour
Rice paper
Silver food spray
1 packet red jelly

You will need: plastic cups, rubber
bands, white muffin cases and a
camcorder to record any unusual
activity

## FEEDS

48

# DIRECTIONS

Focus.

Preheat the oven to 200°C (180°C fan/400°F/gas mark 6) and line a muffin tray with paper cases.

Whisk the egg with a fork. Then stir in the milk and oil. Sift the flour into a large bowl, then add the sugar, baking powder and salt. Add the egg mixture to the flour and stir until the flour is moistened. The batter should be lumpy. Do not overmix. Fill a tray of the muffin cases two thirds full. Bake for 20–25 minutes or until golden brown. Once cooked, tip the muffins out on to a rack and leave to cool completely.

To make the buttercream icing, whisk the butter in a large bowl until soft. Gently add half the icing sugar and whisk until smooth. Add the remaining icing sugar with a little milk, adding more as necessary to make light fluffy icing. Add the pink food colouring little by little, and mix until well combined.

Really, really focus. Use a knife to apply the buttercream to the cupcakes. Add chocolate sprinkles to create the hairline. Use a sharp knife to cut the liquorice into short strands and fix to the buttercream. Use a paintbrush to apply white food colour to the strawberry laces and thread the laces through the mini marshmallows.

Using a fine paintbrush, apply the black food colour to the chocolate buttons to create the slits of the eyes and pupils. Next, apply purple food colouring to colour the eyelids. Use a little melted chocolate to affix the decorated buttons to the face of the cupcake.

Follow the instructions on the packet to prepare the jelly and set aside to cool. Crumple a plastic cup, taking care not to split it, and use a rubber band to hold it in place. Pour in the cooled jelly and leave in the fridge to set.

To create the lid and ring pull for the cola can, use a sharp knife to cut a shape from the rice paper and colour with the food spray.

Once the jelly is set, remove from the plastic cup and apply the lid. Meanwhile, melt the white chocolate buttons very gently over hot water. Once melted, use a small piping bag and nozzle to apply decoration to the can's exterior.

It's over! As unpleasant as that might have been, it's not like you would ever be forced to kill a cat or anything horrific like tha– Oh.

# STRANGER FILLINGS

## PLAYERS MANUAL

## FANTASY ROLE PLAYING GAME

# JOYCE'S CLOSE CALL

**DIFFICULTY**

## The original dine and dash, these treats spell danger

## INGREDIENTS

**FOR THE BISCUITS**
280g/10oz plain flour
200g/7oz butter, firm
100g/4oz icing sugar
2 egg yolks
1 tsp vanilla extract

**TO DECORATE**
100g/4oz icing sugar
1 egg white
Yellow, black and brown food colour
1 packet chocolate peanut sweets

You will need: a circular biscuit cutter and ideally R– U– and N– shaped cutters (though you can use a sharp knife instead)

**FOR THE CAKE**
300g/10½oz butter
400g/14oz sugar
6 eggs, lightly beaten
350g/12oz self-raising flour
100g/4oz cocoa powder, sieved
3–4 tbsp milk

**FOR THE BUTTERCREAM**
125g /5oz butter, softened
250g /10oz icing sugar
1–2 tbsp milk
Strawberry or raspberry jam
500g/1lb 2oz white ready-to-roll icing
1 packet white chocolate sticks
Black, red and yellow food colour
100g/4oz melted white chocolate

You will need: a fine paintbrush

## FEEDS

53

# DIRECTIONS

## FOR THE BISCUITS:

Put the flour in a bowl. Cut the butter into small pieces and add to the flour.

Rub the butter into the flour with your fingertips until the mix looks like breadcrumbs. Add the sugar, egg yolks and vanilla extract and mix to a dough. Put it into a plastic bag and chill for at least 30 minutes.

Roll out the dough on a lightly floured surface to about 5mm (0.25 inch) thickness. Cut out shapes with the circular cutter, and also the three letters using cutters or a sharp knife and place them on a baking sheet lined with baking parchment. Put them back into the fridge to chill for 30 minutes.

Meanwhile, preheat the oven to 180°C (160°C fan/350°F/gas mark 4).

Bake the biscuits for 12–15 minutes, until they are beginning to brown around the edges. (The letters will cook much more quickly than the biscuits, so keep an eye on them.) Remove from the oven and allow to cool on the sheet before carefully lifting off.

Sieve the icing sugar into a small bowl and add a little egg white little by little, whisking well until a flooding consistency is reached. Set aside roughly one quarter of the icing mix and add black food colour. Use a wooden spoon to flood the letters as shown.

Next, add the yellow food colour to the remaining icing and flood the biscuits over a wire rack until a smooth, even surface is achieved.

Use a paintbrush to add the black, yellow and brown food colour to make the wallpaper decoration.

Use a small piping bag and nozzle to apply the black wiring to the biscuits and affix red, blue and green peanut sweets using a little leftover icing.

Finally, use a paintbrush to apply red, green and blue food colour as shown.

# DIRECTIONS CONTINUED

## FOR THE CAKE

Preheat the oven to 175°C (160°C fan/325°F/gas mark 4). Grease and line a deep 34 x 23cm (13 x 9 inch) rectangular baking tin. Cream the butter and sugar until pale in colour, light and fluffy. Add the eggs very gradually, whisking well between each addition. Fold the flour and cocoa powder into the mix until blended. Add enough milk to give a dropping consistency and spoon into the prepared tin, smoothing the top and making a slight dip in the centre. Bake for 45–55 minutes, or until firm to the touch and a knife inserted in the centre comes out clean. Cool in the tin for a few minutes, then turn out on to a rack to cool completely.

To make the buttercream icing, whisk the butter in a large bowl until soft. Gently add half the icing sugar and whisk until smooth. Add the remaining icing sugar with a little milk, adding more as necessary to make a light fluffy icing.

Use a knife to cut the cake in half and then add buttercream between the two halves along with the jam.

Use a knife to cut the white chocolate fingers to the correct length and use a little melted chocolate to affix them to the outside of the cake.

Use the chocolate sticks to form the shape of the claw, using a little melted chocolate to hold them together. Once complete, use a paintbrush to decorate with red and black food colour and then insert into the top of the cake.

Roll out almost all of the icing, adding a little of the yellow food colour as required, on a floured surface and then drape over the cake and claw, allowing the icing to tear and the claw to penetrate.

Add yellow food colour to the remaining icing and fashion the telephone, as shown.

Use the paintbrush to apply the black and yellow food colouring to create the wallpaper pattern.

Now get out of the house as quickly as you can and try not to think about how much it will cost to have the wallpaper redone.

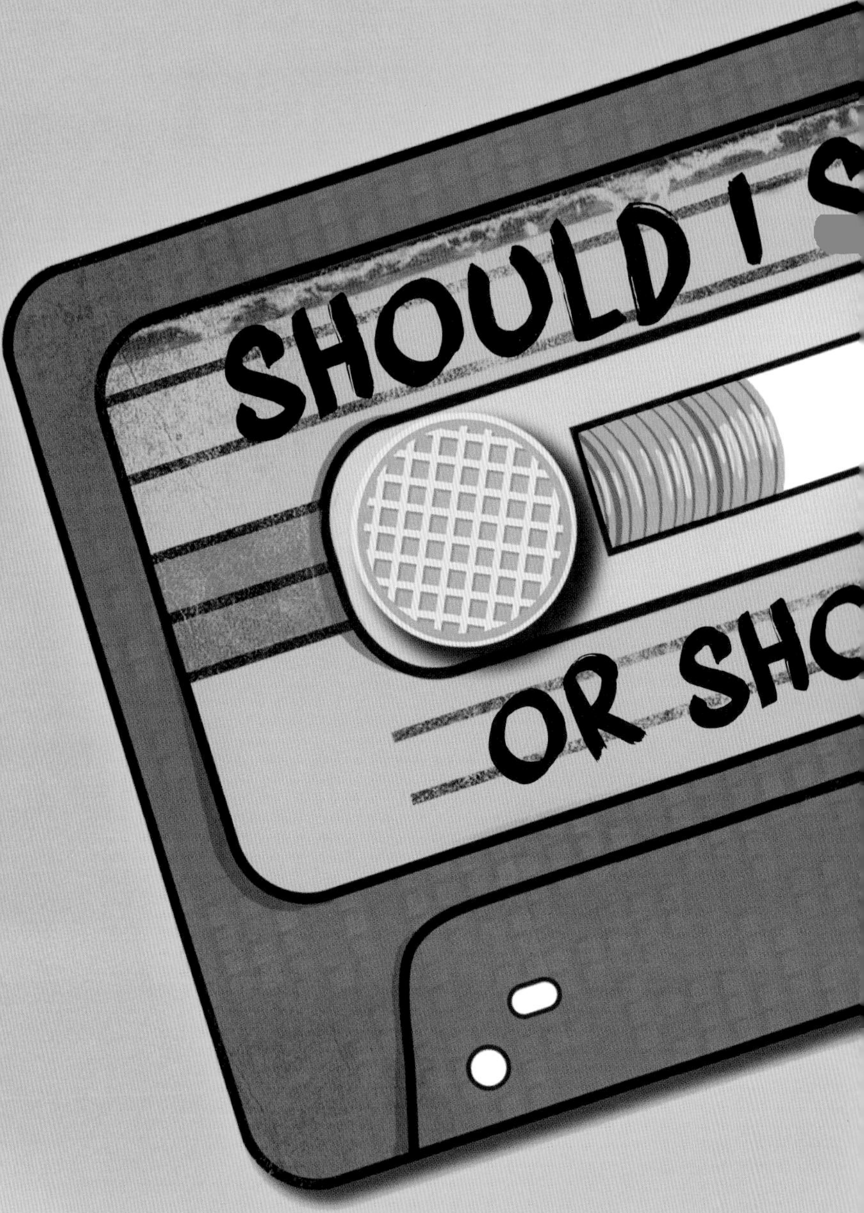
SHOULD I S
OR SHO

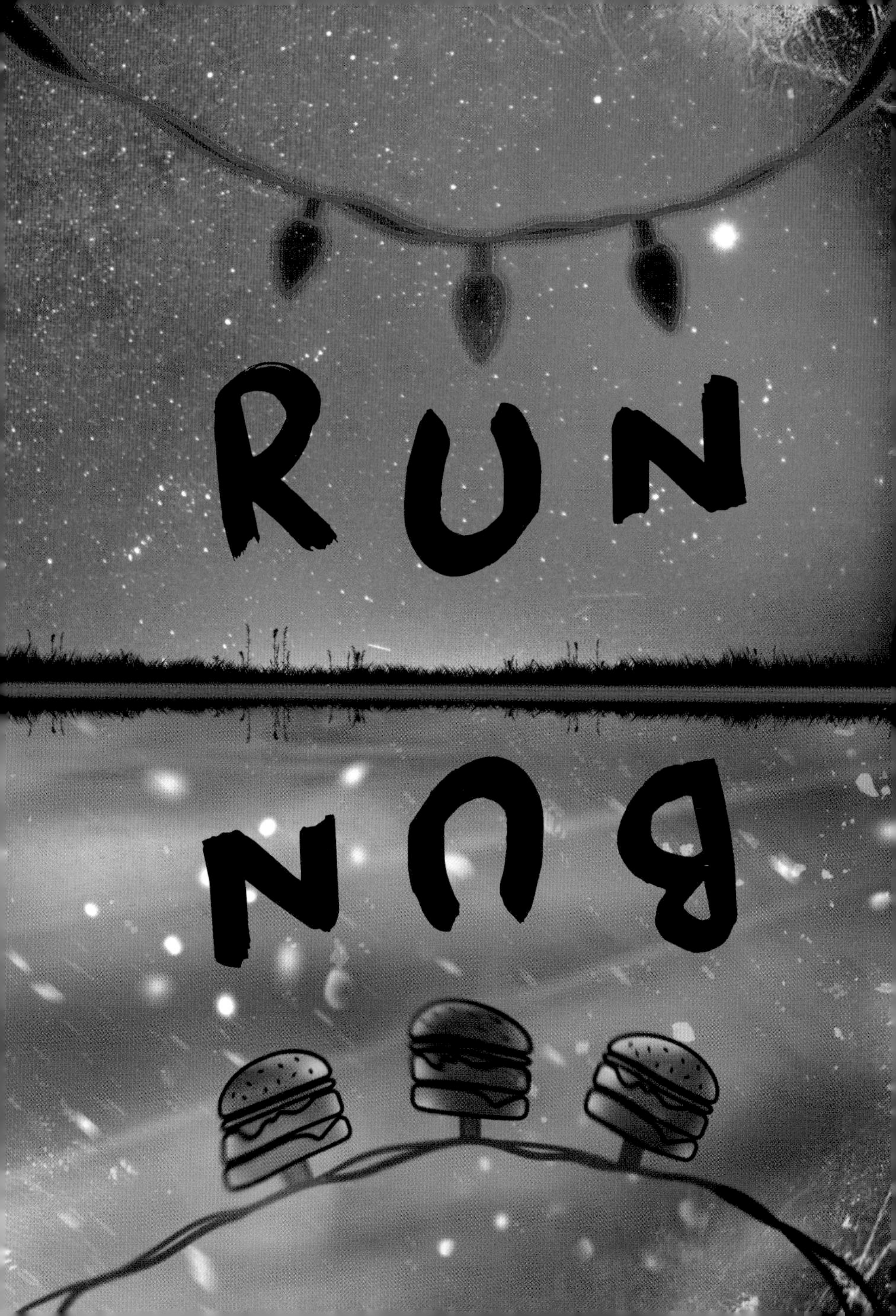
RUN

# WILL'S FAKE CAKE

## A familiar face with a very surprising stuffing

## INGREDIENTS

**FOR THE BRIOCHE**
100ml/3½fl oz warm water
1 tsp dried yeast
2 tbsp warm milk
1 tbsp caster sugar
225g/8oz strong bread flour, plus extra for dusting
½ tsp salt
30g/1oz butter
1 large egg, lightly beaten, plus 1 egg yolk for glazing

**FOR THE REST**
1 packet white marshmallows
250g/9oz milk chocolate
Black food colour
Blue ready-to-roll icing

You will need: a gingerbread man shaped cutter, a piping bag
with a small nozzle, and a paintbrush

## FEEDS

64

# DIRECTIONS

To make the brioche, mix the warm water, yeast, warm milk and sugar in a bowl. Let it stand for 5 minutes until it begins to froth up. Mix the flour and salt together in a large mixing bowl, and rub in the butter until the mixture resembles fine breadcrumbs. Make a well in the centre and add the yeast mixture and the beaten egg.

Use your hands to mix it into a very sticky dough, adding just enough flour to make it workable. Tip the dough out on to a floured work surface and knead well for 10 minutes until it feels a little elastic – it will still be very sticky but don't be tempted to add too much flour. Place in an oiled bowl, cover with cling film and set aside to rise for 2–3 hours or until doubled in size.

Tip out on to the floured work surface and knead again for 2 minutes. The dough should be much less sticky now, but add a little flour if it needs it. Press the dough out into a rectangle roughly 25 x 15cm (10 x 6 inches).

Using a man-shaped cutter, cut out the boy. Place him on to a greased baking sheet, cover lightly with oiled cling film and leave for about 1 hour or until doubled in size again.

Preheat the oven to 200°C (180°C fan/350°F/gas mark 6). Whisk the egg yolk with a little water and brush over the brioche shape. Bake for 20–30 minutes or until golden, then place on a rack to cool.

Once cooled, flip over the brioche figure and get a sharp knife ready. Take a deep breath because this next bit is going to be unpleasant. Cut out the back of the torso and remove some of the brioche. Insert as many marshmallows as you can before replacing the back and carefully turn the brioche figure over, keeping the back intact.

Use the knife to cut a hole in the front of the figure and carefully tease out some of the marshmallow so it sticks out.

To make the hair, melt the chocolate in a bowl suspended over a pan of simmering water (do not allow the bottom of the bowl to touch the water), then allow it to cool a little before adding it to the piping bag and nozzle and piping the strands of hair on.

Use a paintbrush to apply the black food colour for the eyes and mouth.

Roll out the icing, using flour on the surface and on the rolling pin, and shape into the blanket.

Tease out the stuffing with a mixture of relief and horror, as you realise those pesky kids might be on to something.

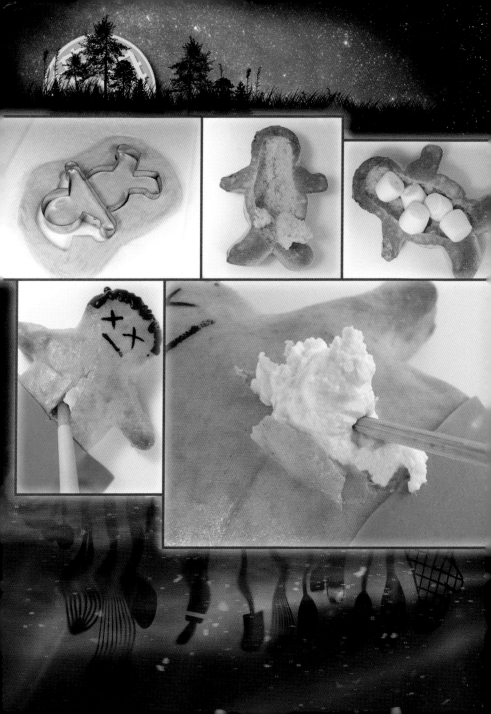

# CAKE BYERS

## Go to your special place with this delicious shack of a snack

## INGREDIENTS

**FOR THE CAKE**
300g/10oz butter, softened
400g/14oz sugar
6 medium eggs, lightly beaten
350g/12oz self-raising flour
100g/3½oz cocoa powder, sifted
90ml/3fl oz milk

**FOR THE BUTTERCREAM**
450g/1lb icing sugar, sifted
250g/9oz butter, softened
1–2 tbsp milk
Brown food colour

**FOR THE EDIBLE SOIL**
100g/4oz caster sugar
2 tbsp water
70g/2½oz plain chocolate, chopped
  into pieces

**TO DECORATE:**
Orange food colour
Ice-cream wafers
150g/5½oz milk chocolate
1 packet chocolate sticks
Rice paper
Brown, red, yellow and
  blue food colour
150g milk chocolate
Chocolate cream biscuit, circular
White chocolate stars

You will need: a paintbrush, a piping
bag with a small, plain nozzle and a
small circular biscuit cutter

## FEEDS

68

# DIRECTIONS

Remember, you're not like other kids. Preheat the oven to 180°C (160°C fan assisted/350°F/gas mark 4). Grease and line a 20cm (8 inch) round baking tin.

Cream the butter and sugar until pale, light and fluffy. Add the eggs gradually, whisking well between each addition. Combine the flour and cocoa powder, then fold into the mix until blended. Add enough milk to give a dropping consistency and spoon into the prepared tin, smoothing the top and making a slight dip in the centre. Bake for 45–55 minutes, or until firm to the touch and a knife inserted in the centre comes out clean. Cool in the tin for a few minutes, then turn out on to a rack to cool completely.

For the buttercream, whisk the icing sugar and butter together until light and fluffy, adding a little milk if needed. Add the brown food colour and stir until it is the correct shade. Spread the icing in a thick, even layer on top of the cake.

For the edible soil, heat the sugar and water in a pan and insert a sugar thermometer. When it reaches 130°C/266°F, take off the heat. If you haven't got a thermometer, wait until all the sugar is dissolved and starting to change to a medium brown colour. Add the chocolate and stir with a whisk for 1 minute, making sure it is all coated. Empty the mixture on to a piece of foil to cool. Once cooled, spread the soil evenly on to the cake.

To make the leaves, use a paintbrush to apply the orange food colour to the wafers. Leave to dry and then use scissors to cut into small pieces before using your hands to crumble it into tiny pieces. Sprinkle some of this on to the edible soil on the cake.

To make the tree branches, melt the chocolate very gently over hot water. Leave to cool for a few minutes before transferring to the piping bag. Pipe the tree shapes on to some baking parchment. Carefully add some of the crushed-up 'leaves' then chill until firm. At the same time, use a knife to smear some chocolate on the parchment to make the sign.

Construct the fort by placing the chocolate sticks into the cake and using some of the melted chocolate to fix them together. Remove the trees from the fridge and place them on top of the completed fort.

Cut a sheet of edible paper and use a paintbrush to decorate with the food colours and do the same to the chocolate sign. To make the tyre, halve the chocolate biscuit and use a circular cutter moistened with a little milk to slowly remove the centre. To make the flag, use a paintbrush to decorate the rice paper and then add the chocolate stars.

Mom is coming to get you, so just hold on and try not to eat too many slugs in the meantime.

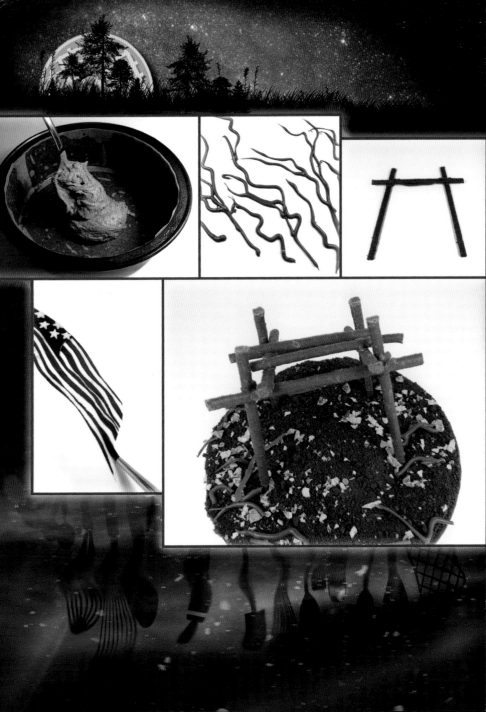

# JANE IVES' DELICIOUS DIVE

DIFFICULTY

## Let your mind wander with this submersible snack

### Ingredients

2 packets green jelly
25g/1oz butter
150g/6oz mini marshmallows
85g/3oz crisped rice cereal
200g/7oz white chocolate
Brown/caramel food colour
25g/1oz dark chocolate
Cola laces
Yellow food spray

You will need: a tube-shaped glass or jar, a small can,
a toothpick and a cake pop stick

## FEEDS

# DIRECTIONS

Prepare the green jelly, following the directions on the packet and pour into the receptacle before leaving in the fridge to set.

Grease a 32 x 23cm (13 x 9 inch) baking tray. Melt the butter in a large heavy-based saucepan over a low heat. Add the marshmallows and cook gently until they are completely melted and blended, stirring constantly. Mix well. Take the pan off the heat and immediately add the cereal, mixing lightly until well coated. Let the mix cool before shaping into a head and a body, as shown. It will be very sticky, so wet your hands if necessary.

For the chocolate coating, place the white chocolate in a heatproof bowl and set over a pan of simmering water, stirring occasionally until just melted. Remove from the heat. Dip the head and body in the melted chocolate to create an even covering and place in the fridge to cool.

Apply baking parchment to the can and use a knife to apply melted chocolate. Once it has begun to cool, use the knife to trim the rough edges to create the shape of the diving helmet and place it in the fridge.

Add the food colour to the remaining melted chocolate.

To create the hand, pipe on to some baking parchment and leave to cool just long enough to harden slightly. Remove it from the parchment and use a toothpick to stick it to the inside of your receptacle, before placing the whole thing in the fridge.

Once the head and body have cooled, use a toothpick to apply melted white chocolate and then dark chocolate to create the face.

Once completely cooled, remove the diving suit shape from the can and fix to the head and body using a little melted chocolate and place the entire thing in the fridge to cool.

To create the air tube, use the yellow food spray to colour one of the laces and use a little melted chocolate to fix it to the body.

Place the figure in the jelly and leave to fully set in the fridge.

Wave goodbye to Papa as you sink in. Your world is about to turn upside down!

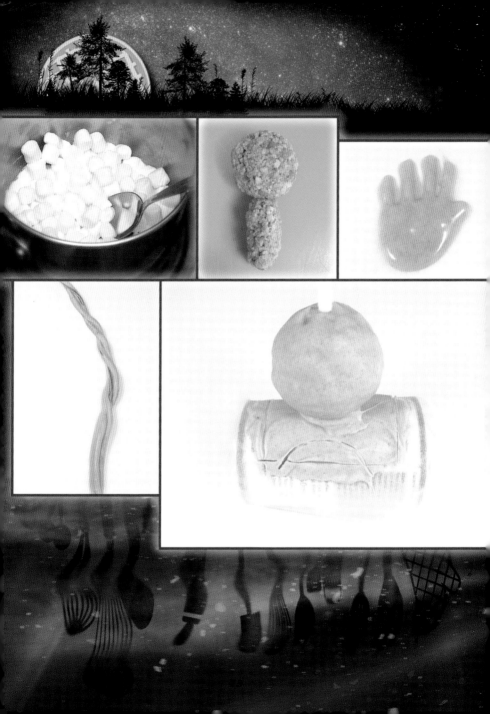

BAKE ON
THROUGH
TO THE
OTHER SIDE!

# EL'S TELEPATHIC TART

## (WITH RUSSIAN DRESSING)

**DIFFICULTY**

A cold war classic. Take a trip to the other side with these transporting treats

## INGREDIENTS

**FOR THE CHOCOLATE CAKE**
100g/3½oz margarine, plus extra
   for greasing
25g/1oz cocoa powder, plus extra
   for dusting
3 tbsp boiling water
100g/3½oz caster sugar
100g/3½oz self-raising flour
1 level tsp baking powder
2 large free-range eggs

**FOR THE MOUSSE**
300g/10oz plain chocolate (no more
   than 40–50 per cent cocoa solids),
   broken into squares
450ml/16fl oz whipping cream

**FOR THE MIRROR GLAZE**
15g/½oz gelatin powder
80ml/3fl oz cold water
1½ tbsp water
200g/7oz white granulated sugar
200g/7oz glucose or golden syrup
150g/5oz sweetened condensed milk
200g/7oz chocolate
Black gel food colour

**FOR THE FIGURES**
White ready-to-roll icing
Chocolate sprinkles
Pink, khaki and blue food colour

## FEEDS

# DIRECTIONS

Head towards the guy with the funny hat. Preheat the oven to 180°C (160°C fan/350°F/gas mark 4). Grease the tin with margarine and line the base and sides with baking parchment. You need to line the tin right to the top.

For the chocolate cake, measure the cocoa powder into a large bowl. Pour over the boiling water and mix to a paste with a spatula. Add the rest of the dry ingredients and the eggs and margarine. Whisk until smooth using a handheld mixer.

Spoon the mixture into the prepared cake tin and level the surface with a palette knife. Bake in the oven for 20–25 minutes, or until a skewer inserted into the centre of the cake comes out clean. This would be easier if you had a basic grasp of Russian.

Meanwhile, for the mousse, place the chocolate in a bowl and melt over a pan of gently simmering water (do not allow the bowl to touch the water). Stir continuously, taking care not to let the chocolate get too hot. Set aside to cool a little. Whip the cream until soft peaks form. Carefully fold in the melted chocolate until smooth and not streaky.

When the cake has cooled, spoon the chocolate mousse on top in the tin and level with a palette knife. Cover the tin with cling film and chill in the fridge for a minimum of 4 hours, until the mousse is firm.

To make the mirror glaze, bloom the gelatin in cold water and allow to sit. Break the chocolate into small pieces and place in a large bowl, ready for the glaze. Boil water, sugar and glucose in a saucepan over a medium heat until fully dissolved. Remove the pan from the heat, then add in the gelatin and condensed milk. Wait... What was that noise?!

Pour the entire warm mixture over the chocolate. Add the black food colour and stir until the right colour is achieved. Allow to sit for 5 minutes. Stir the mix carefully, then use a thermometer to see when the temperature reaches 32°C/90°F and is ready for pouring.

Cover a surface or rimmed baking sheet with cling film for easy clean-up. You want to be able to pour and have the excess run off. To finish, take a long offset spatula and hold it perfectly level to the top. Swipe the spatula across the top of the cake, just barely above the cake level to remove excess. This will leave your finish looking flat and perfect. Allow to sit before moving the cake.

Roll out the icing to create the figures. Use the chocolate sprinkles to decorate the man's hat and use food colour and a small paintbrush to apply their features. Use toothpicks to place them in the cake. Scream with horror as the kitchen walls crumble and your guests scramble for safety.

# FRIENDSHIP BITES

**Friends don't lie, but they sure do taste good**

## INGREDIENTS

50g/2oz butter
300g/12oz mini marshmallows
175g/6oz crisped rice cereal
100g/4oz milk chocolate
100g/4oz white chocolate
100g/4oz red chocolate or candy melts,
　all in drops or broken into pieces
(You will need energy for your travels)

TO DECORATE
Dark chocolate sprinkles
Edible paper
Green and black food colour
Cola laces
Red, blue and white ready-to-roll icing
Petal paste

You will need: cake-pop sticks

## FEEDS

# DIRECTIONS

Grease a 32 x 23cm (13 x 9 inch) baking tin.

Melt the butter in a large heavy-based saucepan over a low heat. Add the marshmallows and cook gently until they are completely melted and blended, stirring constantly. Mix well. Take the pan off the heat and immediately add the cereal, mixing lightly until well coated.

Let the mix cool before dividing into three equal portions and shaping each into a head. It will be very sticky, so wet your hands if necessary. Once complete, use a sharp knife to cut the upper quarter from one of the heads. Set aside this offcut for later. Use a knife to make a small hole in the base of each of the heads. (Remember the rule 'If you draw first blood...') Insert the cake-pop sticks with a little melted chocolate. Place the three heads upright in a freezer to harden.

For the chocolate coatings, place the milk chocolate in a heatproof bowl and then the white and red chocolate combined in a separate heatproof bowl. Set both over a pan of simmering water, stirring occasionally until just melted and mixing the red and white chocolate to make a pink. Don't let the water boil, unless you're a goblin with an intelligence score of zero.

Remove both from the heat and use a palette knife to apply the chocolate to one of the heads and the pink mixture to the other two. Using a fine paintbrush, apply the black food colour to create the faces. Set aside a little melted chocolate for decoration.

For Lucas's head, dip the top of the milk chocolate-covered head into a bowl of dark chocolate sprinkles.

Use a knife to cut a strip from the edible paper and then use a paintbrush to apply the green and black food colours to make a camouflage pattern. When dry, wrap the paper around the milk chocolate head to make a bandana.

For Dustin's head, use a sharp knife to cut the cola laces to length and then, using a toothpick, apply a little melted chocolate to the end of the laces to affix them to the head.

Roll out the icing and use a sharp knife to cut the pattern for the cap and lay it on the offcut of the head prepared earlier. To make the peak of the cap you may need to use some petal paste to stiffen the icing. Attach to the head with melted chocolate.

For Mike's head, use a small piping bag and nozzle to pipe the leftover milk chocolate to form the hair.

Share and enjoy. And remember that you CAN have more than one best friend.

# EL FLOTANTE

**Harnessing the awesome power of jello, this powerful pud will heighten your senses**

## INGREDIENTS

**FOR THE SPONGE**
60g/2oz self-raising flour
60g/2oz butter, at room temperature
60g/2oz caster sugar
1 egg (not Eggo)
½ tsp baking powder

**FOR THE TRIFLE**
Gelatin (enough for 2 pints of water)
Blue food colour
50g/2oz chocolate (white or milk)
Sponge fingers

**TO DECORATE**
300ml/½ pint custard
Pink food colour
It helps to have a crackly radio
  on the side.
One packet marshmallows
60g/2oz dark chocolate

You will need: a 'tank'-shaped
receptacle, a toothpick, a piping
bag and nozzle and a gingerbread
man (or even better, woman) cutter.
You may find this treat gets mistaken
for being a boy, though.

## FEEDS

# DIRECTIONS

Find an empty school and fill a paddling pool with room-temperature water.

Prepare the gelatin as directed on the packet and add some blue food colour. Put it in the fridge to speed up cooling, but don't let it set.

Preheat the oven to 180°C (160°C fan/350°F/gas mark 4). Place the ingredients for the sponge cake into a large bowl and mix together with a hand-held electric mixer.

Pour the mixture out onto a non-stick tray and place in the oven for 15–20 minutes until golden brown. Cool on a wire rack.

Once cooled, use the cutter to cut out a shape (and more than one if you can).

Warm some of the chocolate gently over a pan of warm water and use the melted chocolate to stick the sponge fingers to the bottom of the receptacle.

Pour the jelly on top of the sponge fingers and place the bowl in the fridge to set.

Apply the pink food colour to the custard to turn it the desired shade of pink for the dress.

Add a little custard to a piping bag and pipe the outline shape of the dress. Use the remaining custard to fill in the outline, using a knife if necessary to spread the custard evenly.

Use a toothpick to apply the marshmallows and a sharp knife to cut the goggles from the icing. Finally fill a piping bag with a little chocolate and pipe on the mouth.

Now it's time to go and see Will, so dive in!

# MONSTER–HUNTING MEDLEY

## Prepare for a bite-sized battle with these deadly delights

### INGREDIENTS

**TO MAKE THE BASEBALL BAT**
25g/1oz butter
150g/6oz mini marshmallows
85g/3oz crisped rice cereal
80g/3oz milk chocolate and 50g/1¾oz
    of dark chocolate, in drops or
    broken into pieces (just like Steve
    and Nancy's relationship)
Chocolate sticks
Silver food spray

**TO MAKE THE PETROL CAN**
80g red candy melts
Marshmallow and chocolate teacakes
Cola laces
Chocolate sticks
Silver food spray
Silver food colour

**TO MAKE THE BEAR TRAP**
1 packet chewy sweet bars
Strawberry laces
Black food spray

You may also need: four
boxes of .38 calibre rounds

## FEEDS

94

# DIRECTIONS

## TO MAKE THE BASEBALL BAT:
Grease a 32 x 23cm (13 x 9 inch) baking tray. Melt the butter in a large
heavy-based saucepan over low heat. Add the marshmallows and cook
gently until they are completely melted and blended, stirring constantly.
Mix well. Take the pan off the heat and immediately add the cereal,
mixing lightly until well coated. Let the mix cool before shaping into a
bat. It will be very sticky, so wet hands if necessary.

Place the two chocolates in separate heatproof bowls and set over a pan
of simmering water, stirring occasionally until just melted. Remove from
the heat and use a palette knife to apply to the exterior of the bat: first
the milk chocolate, and then brush the darker chocolate on top to create
streaks.

Use a sharp knife to cut the chocolate sticks to make the nails and spray
them silver with the food spray. Use a little melted chocolate to fix them
to the bat. Leave somewhere cool to harden.

## TO MAKE THE PETROL CAN:
Place the red candy melts in a heatproof bowl and set over a pan of
simmering water, stirring occasionally until just melted. Remove
from the heat and use a palette knife to apply to the exterior of the
marshmallow and chocolate teacake.

Use a knife to cut a chocolate stick into the shape of the nozzle and
decorate with melted red candy and a loop of cola lace, decorated with
silver food spray.

## TO MAKE THE TRAP:
Use a sharp knife to cut the chewy sweet bar into the required pattern.
Tie the strawberry laces into loops to form a chain, then apply the black
food spray to the sweets.

For best results, begin with the baseball bat, then move on to the trap,
before finishing things off with the petrol can. (Warning: this doesn't
always work.)

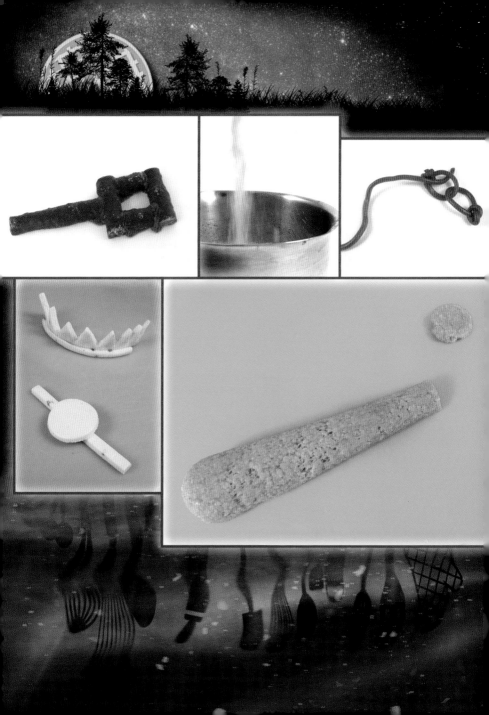

# ELEVEN'S EGGOS

So delicious you won't ever want
to eat anything else!

## INGREDIENTS

Warning: do not steal these ingredients from your local store

150g dark chocolate
1 packet of Eggos
1 banana
1 tsp strawberry jam
1 packet white chocolate buttons
Black food colour

FEEDS

# DIRECTIONS

Melt the dark chocolate in a bowl over a pan of simmering water and dip the Eggo in as shown to create the hairline.

Leave the Eggo in the fridge to cool.

Use a knife to cut a nose from the banana and affix to the Eggo using a little melted chocolate.

Apply some jam with a toothpick or paintbrush. Fix the white buttons on with melted chocolate and use a paintbrush to add the food colour for the eyes.

It's time to eat. Set your treats out on a plate or, for best results, serve them from a box left in the woods.

# MIKE'S ROCK-CAKE RESCUE

**DIFFICULTY**

## You're going to fall for this scenic snack

## INGREDIENTS

2 packets of blue or green jelly
225g/8oz self-raising flour
75g/2½oz caster sugar (not too much,
   unless you want an early trip to the
   dentist)
1 tsp baking powder
125g/4½oz butter, cubed
150g/5½oz dried fruit
1 free-range egg
1 tbsp milk
2 tsp vanilla extract
Digestive biscuits
Green food colour
Chocolate sticks
Ready-to-roll shortcrust pastry
White food colour
Black food colour
60g/2oz chocolate

FOR THE BUTTERCREAM
50g/2oz icing sugar
25g/1oz butter, softened
1–2 tbsp milk

You will need: a toothpick,
a paintbrush

## FEEDS

# DIRECTIONS

Preheat oven to 180°C (160°C fan/350°F/gas mark 4) and line two baking trays with baking parchment.

Prepare the jelly, following the instructions on the packet and pour the mixture into a heavily oiled receptacle before leaving in the fridge to cool. (You want to be able to easily tip it out later.)

Mix the flour, sugar and baking powder in a bowl and rub in the cubed butter until the mixture looks like breadcrumbs, then mix in the dried fruit.

In a clean bowl, whisk the egg and milk together with the vanilla extract.

Add the egg mixture to the dry ingredients and stir with a spoon until the mixture just comes together as a thick lumpy dough.

Divide the mixture into four or five tiers to make the curved walls of the gorge and place onto the prepared baking trays. Leave space between them as they will flatten and spread out to double their size during baking.

Bake for 15–20 minutes, until golden brown. Remove the cakes from the oven, allow to cool for a couple of minutes, then turn them out onto a wire rack to cool.

To make the buttercream, whisk the icing sugar and butter together until light and fluffy, adding a little milk if necessary. Add the green food colour and stir until the correct colour is achieved. Fill out a piping bag with nozzle and pipe the buttercream around shortened pieces of chocolate sticks to create trees and tree trunks.

To make the vegetation, crush the biscuits to a fine crumble

using a tea towel and rolling pin, or a blender, and add some green food colour.

To make the figure, roll out some of the pastry and use a sharp knife to create the shape of Mike's body. Using a paintbrush,

apply the edible foor colour. Bake for 10–15 minutes or until the edges begin to turn brown. Use a little melted chocolate to affix the figure to a toothpick and insert into the cake.

Tip the jelly out of the receptacle and place in between the rock cakes. Decorate with the chocolate trees and biscuit crumble.

Once finished, fall to the floor exhausted and lament how it was you who opened the gate in the first place.

# FRIENDS DON'T LI(M)E PIE

## A formidable flan that will make your guests flip

### INGREDIENTS

1 packet ready-to-roll shortcrust pastry
Flour, to dust
1 400g/14oz tin sweetened condensed milk
4 large egg yolks
120ml/4fl oz cup fresh lime juice
    (from about 450g/1lb of limes)
1 tsp lime zest, grated
475ml/16fl oz heavy/double cream
Black, blue, white and green food colour

You will need: skewers, toothpicks,
paintbrush, edible glue

## FEEDS

# DIRECTIONS

Go, go, go, go, go, go, go!

To prepare the pastry, dust the work surface lightly with flour. Put two thirds of pastry on it and sprinkle a little flour on top. Avoid using more flour than you need as the pastry will become too dry. Use your rolling pin to press down on the pastry, making little grooves. Turn 90 degrees and repeat until the pastry is about twice its original diameter.

Sprinkle a little more flour underneath if necessary and begin to roll out the pastry gently, turning every so often until it's large enough to fit your tin with a slight overhang. Place the rolling pin at the far end of the pastry and flip it over the rolling pin. Put the pastry into the tin, topside down. Once the pastry is gently laid over, push it into the tin with your hands. Use a small bag of the excess pastry to help push the pastry into the corners. Trim the edges.

Roll out the remaining pastry and use a sharp knife to create the shapes of the trees, bicycles and van. Using a paintbrush, paint the trees, figures and van in food colour. Then bake for 10–15 minutes or until the edges begin to turn brown.

Add the condensed milk, egg yolks, lime juice and zest to a large bowl and mix thoroughly. Pour into the prepared pie crust then bake for 15 minutes, or until set. Allow to cool, then refrigerate for at least 4 hours, but preferably overnight.

When ready to serve, whisk the cream until it holds stiff peaks. Using a spatula, evenly spread the whipped cream on top of the pie and garnish with additional lime zest, if desired.

To assemble, press the trees and figures into the cooked pie's surface (use toothpicks for extra stability if necessary).

Attach one or two large wooden skewers to the back of the van with a little melted chocolate, or edible glue. Pierce the pie with the skewers and position the van so it hovers over the figures.

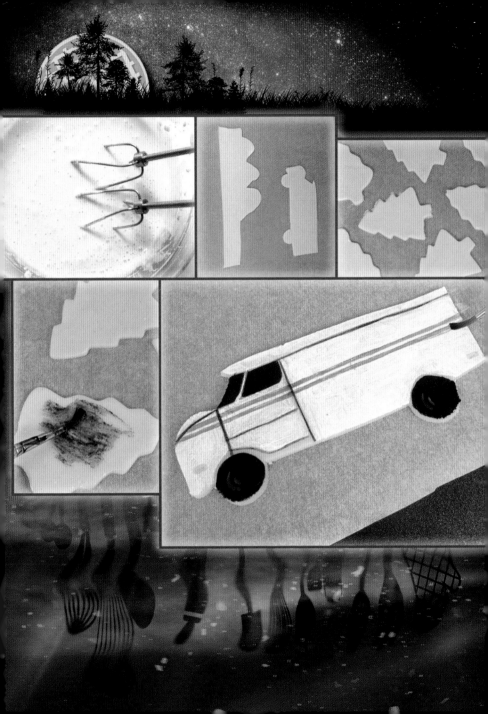

# THE UPSIDE DOWN CAKE

DIFFICULTY

## Cross over to the other side with this inter-dimensional delight

### INGREDIENTS

300g/1lb 2oz butter
400g/14oz sugar
6 eggs, lightly beaten
350g/12oz self-raising flour
100g/3½oz cocoa powder, sieved
3–4 tbsp milk

**FOR THE BUTTERCREAM**
125g/5oz butter, softened
250g/10oz icing sugar
1–2 tbsp milk
Blue and black food colour
500g/1lb 2oz white ready-to-roll icing
100g/3½oz black ready-to-roll icing

**TO DECORATE**
50g/2oz dark chocolate
1 chocolate egg
Yellow food spray
1 packet chocolate sticks

You will need: a piping bag with
a small regular-shaped nozzle and
four cake stands to support the cake
at each corner. And a hazmat suit.

## FEEDS

# DIRECTIONS

You will need to find your nearest portal. We used the one at Hawkins National but it's worth looking in tree trunks.

Preheat the oven to 175°C (160°C fan/325°F/gas mark 4). Grease and line a deep 34 x 23cm (13 x 9 inches) rectangular baking tin. Cream the butter and sugar until pale in colour, light and fluffy. Add the eggs very gradually, beating well between each addition. Combine the flour and cocoa powder, then fold into the mix until blended. Add enough milk to give a dropping consistency and spoon into the prepared tin, smoothing the top and making a slight dip in the centre. Bake for 45–55 minutes, or until firm to the touch and a knife inserted in the centre comes out clean. Cool in the tin for a few minutes, then turn out on to a rack to cool completely.

Don't be distracted by Barb's corpse.

To make the buttercream icing, whisk the butter in a large bowl until soft. Gently add half the icing sugar and whisk until smooth. Add the remaining icing sugar with a little milk, adding more as necessary to make a light fluffy icing. Add the blue and black food colour little by little, and mix until well combined, and then use a palette knife to apply the icing to the surface of the cake.

To make the trees, place the chocolate in a heatproof bowl and set over a pan of simmering water, stirring occasionally until just melted. Remove from the heat and allow to cool a little before spooning into a piping bag. Pipe the trees on to a piece of baking parchment and leave to cool.

Use a little melted chocolate to carefully affix the trees to the cake's surface.

Use a sharp knife to cut the top from the egg and use the yellow food spray to colour it before fixing it to the icing.

To make the other side of the cake, roll out the white and black icing. First drape the black icing where the hole in the wall will be and then overlay with the white icing across the whole of the cake. Use a sharp knife to cut away as desired and then decorate using a piping bag and melted chocolate.

Use the yellow spray to colour the chocolate sticks to create the rails.

To make the figures, use the remaining ready-to-roll icing with food colour to decorate using a paintbrush as necessary.

Carefully remove any wormlike creatures from your guests' airways and dispatch them with a few well-aimed rounds.

# WILL'S SLUG SURPRISE

**DIFFICULTY**

A meal so good you're going to want to bring it up, again and again

## INGREDIENTS

500g/1lb 2oz white chocolate
250g/9oz pink chocolate
1 packet of strawberry or raspberry jelly
60g/2oz dark chocolate
White chocolate buttons
Black food colour
Some gummy worms
Red food colour
Green food colour
White food colour

You will need: party balloons and a thick paintbrush

## FEEDS

# DIRECTIONS

Don't forget to wash your hands before dinner.

Inflate a balloon to the desired size of your chocolate head. Melt the white and pink chocolate in a bowl over a pan of simmering water. Set the chocolate aside to cool for a moment, before using the brush to paint a layer on the balloon. Leave the chocolate on the balloon to set, before repeating the method until you have made a thick chocolate shell all around the balloon, except at the knot.

In the meantime, dispose of any excess slugs down the plughole.

Use a sharp knife to pop and then remove the balloon.

Leave the chocolate shell in the fridge to harden.

Meanwhile, follow the instructions on the packet of jelly and leave in the fridge to set.

Melt the dark chocolate in a bowl over a simmering pan of water and use the piping bag to pipe on the hair.

Use a little of the melted chocolate to fix on the white chocolate buttons and use a paintbrush to apply the black food colour for the eyes.

Use a paintbrush to decorate the gummy worm with the red, green and white food colour.

Use the knife to carefully cut a hole for the mouth in the chocolate head and spoon in the jelly followed by a gummy worm.

Now take your seat at the table in the knowledge that you haven't truly escaped the upside down... Try to enjoy your Christmas dinner though.

Great recipes. No meth-in around.

# Baking Bad

99.1%
PURE
100%
EDIBLE

## WALTER WHEAT

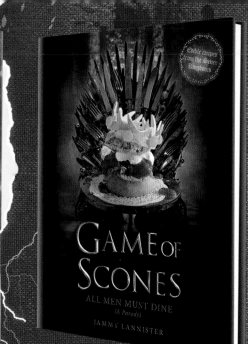

Edible recipes
from the Seven
Kingdoms

# GAME OF SCONES

### ALL MEN MUST DINE
(A Parody)

JAMMY LANNISTER

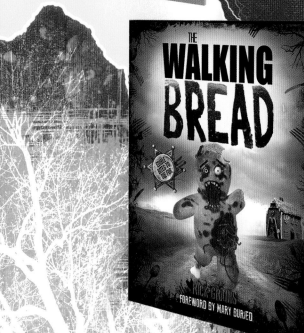

## THE
# WALKING
# BREAD

EDIBLE BITES TO DIE FOR

RICK GRAINS

FOREWORD BY MARY BURIED

# FOLLOW US

@strangerfillings

themuffinbrothers

@strangerfilling

# Author's Note

This book is a loving tribute from a fan and not intended to lay claim to the genius creations of the TV show on which it comments. I love *Stranger Things* and I love baking and this book is my way of paying an homage (and making my own unique comment on the show in the process).

I hope fans will read this book and enjoy reliving moments from the show as they follow the recipes. Who knows, it might even add a new dimension to things!

Bon appetit!

The Author

# WITH THANKS TO...

Anna Valentine
Emma Smith
Mark McGinlay
and all of the team at Trapeze.

# ABOUT THE AUTHORS

The Muffin Brothers are level 14 Dungeons & Dragons wizards, ham radio enthusiasts, and two of the best bakers the 1980s ever saw.

This book was written in conjunction with their mother, using a system of blinking lights.

They divide their time between Indiana and the Upside Down.